Let's Talk About Having a Broken Bone

Elizabeth Weitzman

The Rosen Publishing Group's

PowerKids Press ™

New York

Published in 1997 by The Rosen Publishing Group, Inc.
29 East 21st Street, New York, NY 10010

First Edition

Book Design: Erin McKenna

Photo Illustrations:Front cover by Seth Dinnerman; pp. 4, 7, 8, 11, 12, 16, 19, 20 by Seth Dinnerman; p. 15 © 1992 John Smith/Custom Medical Stock.
Weitzman, Elizabeth.
    Let's talk about having a broken bone / Elizabeth Weitzman.
        p.   cm. — (The Let's talk library)
    Includes index.
    Summary: Describes what happens when you break a bone and how this kind of injury is treated.
    ISBN 0-8239-5028-X (lib.bdg.)
    1. Fractures—Juvenile literature. [1. Fractures. 2. Bones—Wounds and injuries.] I. Title. II. Series.
RD101.W367 1996
    617.1'5—dc20   96-46974
                                                                            CIP
                                                                            AC

Manufactured in the United States of America

Contents

1   Brandon   5

2   Bones   6

3   Fractures   9

4   Do You Have a Broken Bone?   10

5   What Should You Do?   13

6   The Doctor   14

7   Setting the Bone   17

8   Your Cast   18

9   Listen to Your Doctor   21

10   It Will Be Over Soon   22

  Glossary   23

  Index   24

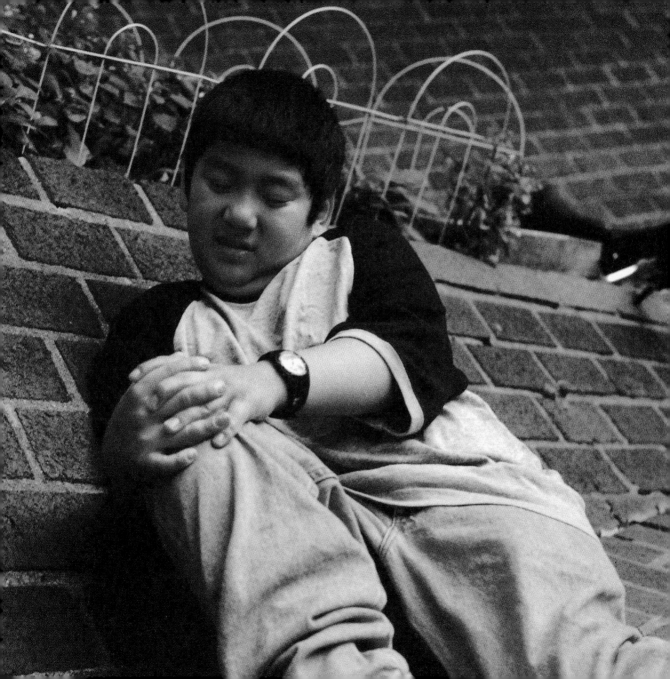

Brandon

One morning Brandon woke up and heard his friends playing outside. He ran down the stairs to join them.

"Be careful!" his dad warned. "I will," Brandon promised.

But just as he ran up to his friends, he slipped on the wet pavement. As Brandon fell he heard an awful "crack." He felt a terrible pain in his leg. Brandon's leg was broken.

◀ Breaking a bone can hurt and be very scary.

Bones

You have 206 bones in your body. These bones make up your **skeleton** (SKEL-uh-ten). Your skeleton is what gives your body its shape. Without it, your body would flop all around like a rag doll's. Bones help you move. They also keep you from moving in ways you shouldn't. When you break a bone, it's because the bone was forced to move the wrong way or something hit the bone too hard.

There are 54 bones in the human foot alone. ▶

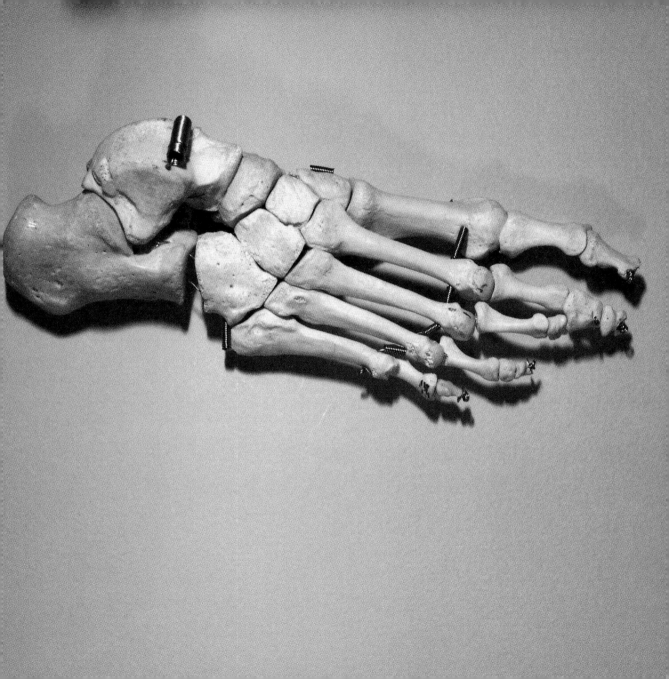

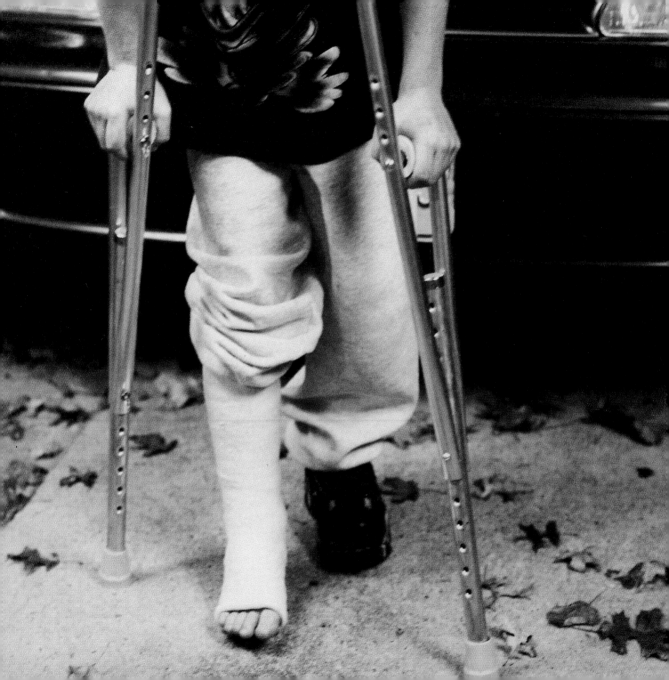

Fractures

When a bone cracks or breaks, it's **fractured** (FRAK-sherd). Have you ever taken a tree branch and bent it in half? Sometimes the branch will break into two pieces. Sometimes it will split without separating all the way. Either of these things can happen to a bone when it fractures. Since you have so many bones, there are many different kinds of fractures.

◀ Most fractures happen in people's wrists, arms, and legs.

Do You Have a Broken Bone?

There are a few ways to know if you've broken a bone. It will hurt a lot and keep on hurting. The area will start to **swell** (SWELL). You may be able to see a piece of the bone sticking out. The place that's hurt may be bent in a weird way. You might also hear a crack or a snap when the bone breaks. But only a doctor can tell for sure if your bone is really broken.

If you have broken a bone, the hurt area may be very paniful. ▶

What Should You Do?

If you think you've broken a bone, you shouldn't move. Stay as still as you can. Don't ever try to fix the bone by yourself. Tell someone to find a grown-up right away. The adult may wrap the hurt area with some clothes or a towel to keep the bone from moving. He will help you get to a **hospital** (HOS-pih-tul) or to a doctor's office.

◀ A grown-up can help you wrap the hurt area until you can get to a doctor.

The Doctor

Everyone who breaks a bone has to see a doctor. There is nothing to be scared of, whether you go to the hospital or to a doctor's office. The doctor will help you get better. It is very important that you tell her exactly how you feel. If you feel faint or sick, you should say so.

You will have to get an **X ray** (EX-ray) of the broken bone. This doesn't hurt at all. The X-ray machine just takes a picture of the fracture.

An X ray will tell the doctor whether your bone is broken or not. ▶

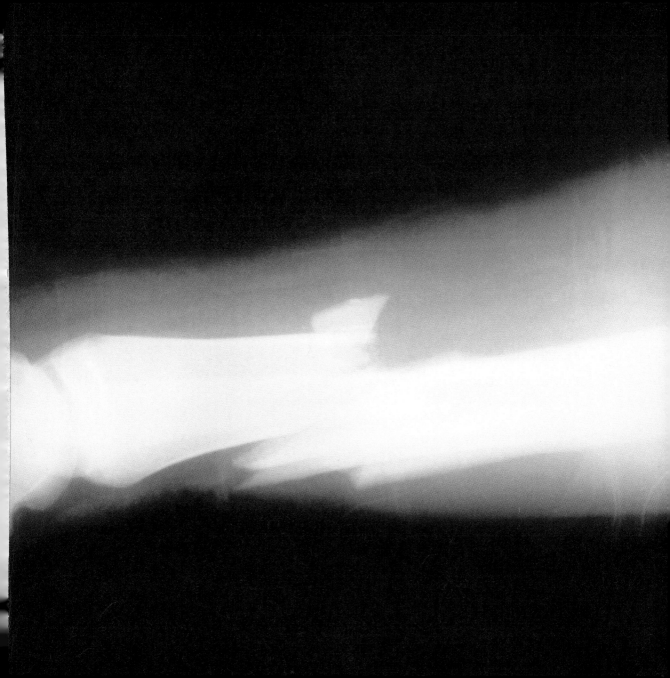

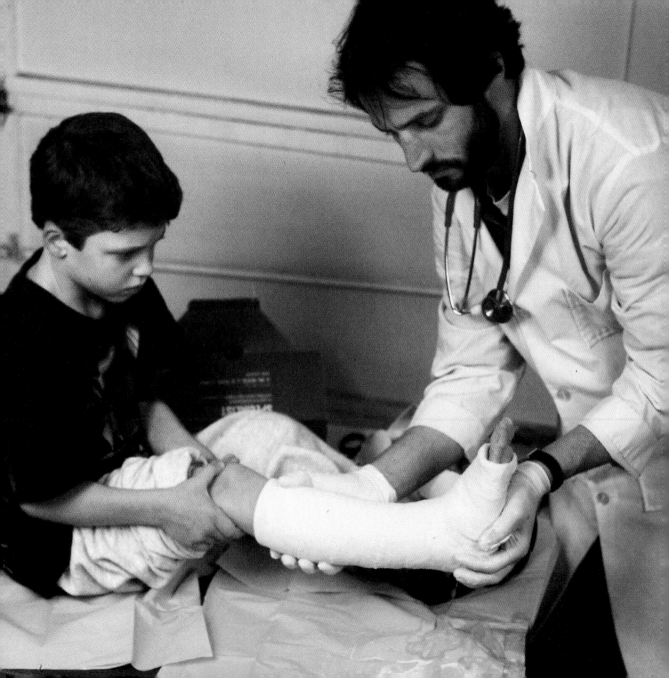

Setting the Bone

As soon as a bone is broken, it starts to **heal** (HEEL). This means that it is growing back together again. A bone has to stay very still to heal well. The doctor will have to **set** (SET) your broken bone. He will put the pieces back where they belong. He may also put the hurt area in a **cast** (KAST) to keep the bone from moving around.

◀ A cast will protect your broken bone while it heals.

Your Cast

If the skin under your cast starts to itch, don't scratch! This could make the hurt area worse. Instead, ask your mom or dad to help. Take a hair dryer and put it on the coolest setting. Aim the air inside your cast. This should help stop the itching.

After four to six weeks, the cast can be removed. The doctor will have to cut it to take it off. The cast-cutter makes a very loud noise and looks a little scary. However, it won't hurt you. It will only touch the cast, not your skin.

Your friends can draw pictures and funny messages on your cast. But you won't miss them when the doctor removes your cast. ▶

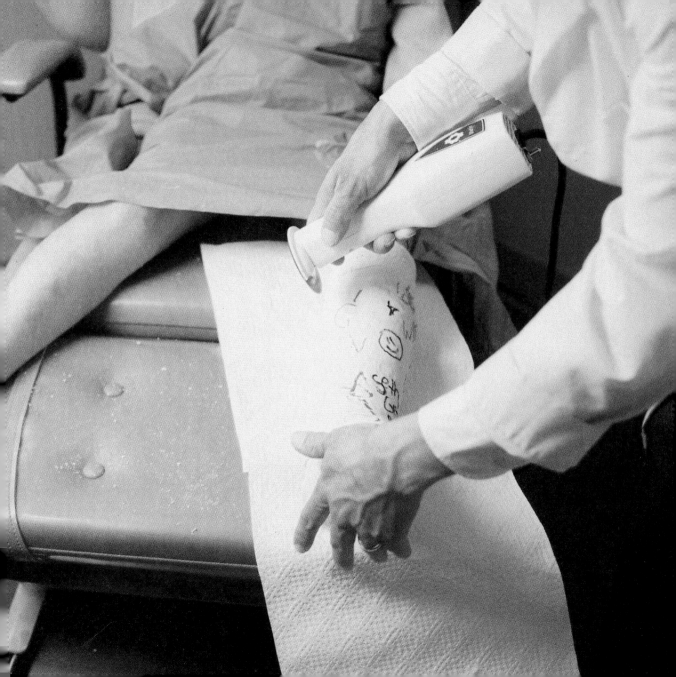

Listen to Your Doctor

It's very important to do whatever your doctor tells you. When she says to keep your cast dry, she means it! And if she says you have to walk with crutches, use them. After a while, you may think you don't really need the crutches anymore. Talk to your doctor before you stop using them. She'll let you know if you can change anything that you were told to do. The more you listen to her, the faster you'll heal.

◀ It's a good idea to do what your doctor tells you until your broken bone is healed.

It Will Be Over Soon

Bones usually heal very well. But it will take some time for you to get better. You may feel bored or angry as you wait for your bone to heal. Try to remember that it will be over soon. Once your bone is healed, it should be as good as new. Soon, you'll be able to play sports, go swimming, and do everything you used to do.

Glossary

cast (KAST) A hard covering for a broken bone that is used to keep the area that is healing still.

fracture (FRAK-sher) Any break in a bone.

heal (HEEL) To get better.

hospital (HOS-pih-tul) Place for the care of the sick or hurt.

set (SET) To put the pieces of a broken bone back in the right position.

skeleton (SKEL-uh-ten) The frame formed by all the bones in your body.

swell (SWELL) To get bigger.

X ray (EX-ray) A picture of part of the inside of your body.

Index

B

bones, 6, 22
  breaking, 9, 10,
    13
broken bones, 5,
    6, 9, 10, 13
  and going to the
    doctor, 14
  setting, 17

C

casts, 17, 18, 21
crutches, 21

D

doctor, 10, 13,
    14, 17, 18,
    21

F

fractures, 9, 14

H

healing, 17, 21,
    22
hospital, 13, 14
hurting, 10

I

itching, 18

S

scratching, 18
setting the bone,
    17
skeleton, 6
sports, 22
swelling, 10

X

X rays, 14